For Shun
and M
with love

NOTES FROM A MOUNTAIN VILLAGE

James

JAMES THORNTON

Also by James Thornton

Nonfiction

Client Earth (with Martin Goodman)

Digging Deeper (with Ben Bundock et al.)

A Field Guide to the Soul

Fiction

Sphinx: the Second Coming

Immediate Harm

Poetry

The Feynman Challenge

NOTES FROM A MOUNTAIN VILLAGE

JAMES THORNTON

BARB
ICAN
PRESS

First published in Great Britain by Barbican Press in 2020

Copyright © James Thornton, 2020

Registered office: 1 Ashenden Road, London E5 0DP

www.barbicanpress.com

@barbicanpress1

Cover by Jason Anscomb
Cover photo by Martin Goodman
Cover calligraphy, of the poem 'A gift of cherries',
by Xi Xiaohong

A CIP catalogue for this book is available from the British
Library

ISBN: 978-1-909954-36-6

Typeset in Palatino

Typeset and Printed in India by Imprint Press

For Martin

Contents

Contents

Acknowledgements

Thanks to Philip Gross for his perceptive, persuasive and elegant editing of this collection;

To the translators Yanqi Zhang and Mengxing Liu, and the reviewer Alicia Liu, for their translation of the poem 'A gift of cherries' into Chinese;

And to our friends and fellow communards, the people of Pézilla-de-Conflent, whose warmth and friendship we have treasured for all these years.

Publisher's note

Poetry is one thread of James's life. In these poems, drawn from twenty-five years of mountain village life, we find the interplay of the natural world and human experience. James brings his capacity as a lawyer to protect that world. So far as we know the universe, nature only has one home: planet Earth. We believe the power of these poems reaches across cultures. In appreciation of James's work with the People's Republic of China, as they seek to usher in a new Ecological Civilization, we commissioned this translation of his poem 'A gift of cherries'.

樱桃之礼

偶遇老农路边独坐
并不熟识

他的腿上
放着古藤编织的篮子

虬结曲折
宛若主人沧桑粗砺的双手

他神色怅惘似乌云笼罩
莫不是值绿蕉红樱之际念茫茫亡妻？

"多美的果实啊" 我不禁上前赞叹
善意拂去了他脸上的阴云

老农缓缓从篮子里捧出一把樱桃
递之与我——"您尝尝吧！"

颗颗饱满的果实仿若精美的漆器
在阳光下闪烁着血液般的浓艳光泽

我连连道谢和他相视一笑
享受着甘美清甜的果实

Wild cherry's pensées

The woman's bent and old and toothless now
when she comes to lift the drainage gate
and send droplets flashing to the river below

Only a few springs since, it seems to me, she
was fresh and lithe and followed by a boy
who grimaced when he ate my sour fruit
and threw the stones at swallows

Ah now, good now, slowly now
with my sap my intelligence rises
and I live again, and soon set bloom
when these cold winds settle down

Then I'll have in bees and wasps and syrphid flies
a hundred light and teasing lovers

Now I'll open, open, relax and I'll open
my sweet white clouds under lapis skies

Fish stock

It was after we'd cleaned
for a week
the house no one
had lived in ten years

walked the hills
violets and hawthorn blooming
where foggy clouds swept through
resolving, as they touched us, into snow

and a horse had joined the cows
by our bend in the river
where the swallows fly low
and we'd drunk the local wine

that the housewarming smell
of fish stock got all the way upstairs
and my body accepted that we are now
here, living, in the nearly untouched Pyrenees

A goathouse in the Pyrenees

When the town was splattered up the hill
by monks five hundred years ago
ours was a goathouse

Stone buildings push up against each other
like embryonic cells hunched in support
our back wall the living rock

Maybe twenty villagers in the winter
summer relatives flocking
to fill the empty houses for August

We've not a single shop
so vans roll in with sausage and pâté
from the butcher over one hill
bread from the baker over another

The goat cheese lady lays out
her museum of decomposition
the fifth and last stage the best

We wondered why it was hard
to understand the old mayor
whose family name is Capulet

out in his fields all day
then we learned French is his third language
after Catalan then Spanish

Twenty-seven

The water sideways lit
like jelly in a sunbeam
its surface transparent
from this height

I counted twenty-seven in the bend
this early morning

they swam by last year's
pomegranates, dry and orange red
on their trees' bare branches

and I wondered if our place
as animals on Earth
won't depend on leaving
the harsh pleasures we admire
to stand in soft wonder with the trout

A gift of cherries

I saw an old villager by the roadside
We'd not spoken before

On his lap a basket made of grapevines
ancient, twisted together

gnarled as his hands
Then a dark cloud moved through him

He might be remembering a dead wife
now it's cherry picking time again

"Hello," I said, "what beautiful cherries"
He roused, cloud gone and said

"Would you like to taste them?"
Then slowly old hands scooped a load

into mine, and they shone in the sun
lacquer suffused with vegetal blood

I thanked him and we smiled
and they were wonderful

The Chapel of St. Felicity

Slowly unmaking itself
for a thousand years
the chapel of St. Felicity

has achieved the perfection
of a tangled grassy bank
where cowslips and violets grow

wild tulip and orchid to follow
and where a drift of sloe
blooming white, beheld a vision:

a swallowtail, newly hatched
black cloisonné and liquid lemon
unfurled its coiled tongue

to let nectar flow up through it
with the pulsebeat of the sun
and not a single thought

Old bones

Because his old bones know
that growing things will in the end
unmake everything we build
the ancient I meet on my morning walk

was standing in the rain today
supporting himself with one hand
against the wall of the house
long vacant, he's lived

across from all his life
and, using his cane
in the other hand, carefully
methodically, extinguishing

every green thing that had
found a purchase in the wall
Looking slowly up, he gave me
an uncomplicated "bonjour!"

Canal

There's a canal not a foot wide
that flows to our house
from the weir at the mill pond

A grating's at this end
before the water breaks
into splinters over the lip of the cliff

Every day this week we've found
frogs against the grating
and rescued them to the river below

Today the cherry's blossoms
dropped wild and white
to coat the canal at water line

like the silk curtains along
the Chinese Emperor's route
and I wonder about the next frog

Bend in the river

In the gorge at the bend in the river
where the gorse runs like yellow fire

up the bank and through the oaks
up to the high schist ridge

and trout swim fat
past the forked sticks in the sand

set for paysans' fishing poles,
a spindrift of flocked seeds

fills the air with gamete snow
as spring pulses into summer

Nos écrivains

The villagers would ask how long
we would stay

At first
they didn't believe our 'three months'

By the third month these good paysans
asked what we did

When we said we were writers
they were overjoyed

"You are writers!" they said
"You are *our* writers!"

Counting beds

The old ladies wondered about our sleeping arrangements
One day the neighbour ran into the house

and upstairs to count the beds, claiming
she needed to see if our toilet worked

After viewing the inherited
multiple beds

She went off to confer with the others
around the bread van

We were both writing books then
and needed space apart

so a friend let us use their extra house
dirty and falling down

We called it 'maison de gloom'
and I'd go there to write and sleep a couple of days at a time

At the bread van
the old ladies asked Martin

"How are things with your copain, he's staying
at the other house

Are you both all right?"

Bernie

To us he was like no other
Bernie we called him, though his name, we learned, was Hugo

He adopted us and when we came to the village
he would know

Show up at the door
happy for pâté, but cheerful without

When the local cat took to jumping on the windowsill
he learned to jump up on the other

Ready always to take a walk
so ready he would know when we set out

We'd sneak out the other side of the village
for the sport of fooling him

but it never worked
He found us, following his preternatural nose

barking, head tipped back
for his joy in our walks in the hills

where the villagers don't go
and his enthusiasm

was the best argument for the villagers
accepting us

Remaining

The air is soft and sweet tonight
and two men have died in the village

One as he hoed in this vineyard
and one in a hospital sleep

The old people gather
comfort the widows

and count the villagers remaining
It's spring, the hills

are fragrant, "and that," says
an old lady friend of ours, "is that"

Across the bridge

Fifty yards behind the cortege
in the brilliance after pelting rain

a boy of five years old comes on
dancing across the bridge in springtime

No fear

Yesterday our neighbour wore a black coverall
over her frock, and carried a basin

of cleaned fragrant trout caught
in the river by her sons

home for the funeral. "He went
in his sleep," she said, the tops of her ears

as red as the veins in her cheek
"And there were six or seven bouquets

for the poor man. I have no fear now
none at all, of living in this house alone

But when the winter comes, perhaps
I shall decide to visit my children"

Hours awake in the night

hours awake in the night
in the spring with the nightingale

he riffs against the pulse
of the mountain stream

I slow down the breath
and hyper clear see

moving down through
deeper shades of emptiness

a darkening series of
Rothko's chapel paintings

see the progression
to death   decide

not yet   await dawn
rhythms

and mountain air

Heart in ice

Heart in ice, I climb
a Pyrenean peak
sit by old basalt
and pray for atonement

"All the ancient twisted karma
every made by me
from beginningless time
through infinite futures
and in this present moment
I now repent for it all"

Deeper and then deeper
the repetitions
while hands touch Earth
for witness and support
When eyes at last open
the world is new:

Lichen and fern
thistle and thyme
pulse full of light
They must always do this
but to see it is forgiveness

Bats

The bats, swallows of the night
surf waves of insects
that roll into the light
above the river by our door:

Flashing close and brief and brown
they merge with their insects
and then, unfolding non-Cartesian
geometries as they go, melt into night

Warblers

Outside my high window
the trees are nearly bare
Easter is early this year

As I walk the hills
I've been struggling to see warblers
migrating up from Africa

They're nimble
at avoiding detection
Warblers are always so

but these have learned
to twist, when you are
sixty feet away, into shadow

From my tree top window though
bare branches offer birds
robins, redstarts and chiffchaff

and then there are serin—small
lemon finches who make the music
of Mediterranean spring

Willow warblers come through
and then another, elegant
in grey with a rusty cap

A black cap, I think, but
the colour of the head is wrong
My field guide tells me

the "female has [a] *rust-coloured* cap"
To know that in this moment
is enough

Golden oriole mating flight

Her in front of me--
how can she be so fast--
yellow and black the whole valley--
stone wall there, away--
three corners turned--
all yellow and black--
flashing, maddening--
fourth corner and back to the oak--
the oak the oak the oak the oak

Banquet

The pig cried out this morning
as they went to catch it

but the banquet
to help pay for

the cancer treatment
of the innkeeper's husband

was put off, as a dinner
with accordion music in the village hall

didn't seem right the week
two other men had died

Spring walk with dog

The mountain called
By the edge of the village, Bernie's bark
then Bernie, eager to join

A windy cool spring day
cistus holding out their
crumpled paper flowers

Halfway to the top I stopped
for orchids and Bernie
ranged around as always

Suddenly he stood stiff at heel
the first time in our life
and I looked up

to see a thin man
rounding the corner
three hundred goats in tow

"It's cold on the top," he said,
"better turn back"
Bernie eager for retreat, we did

Incense

In late spring mountain cold
they burn grapevines
they've pulled from the fields

Smoke like incense fills the village
like the juniper
they burn to buddhas and demons in Tibet

Part of the landscape

There's a place by the river
under ash and linden where

the leaf mould is soft as a feather bed
There in the afternoon heat

slung on the ground between two trunks
my body passes beyond my control

and becomes a part of the landscape
My mind barely touches it

like the sunlight coming green off
the tiger beetle's back as it runs by

Then the body listened
open and listened

to the songs that bathed it round
One commanded my reverie

and would not let me stir:
longing and repose

velvet and dreamlike
passed back and forth in endless variation

by a pair of shy brown birds
I only later knew were nightingales

Wryneck

At dawn the golden oriole flutes us awake
to walk hills above the village

The rising radiation from our star
makes the stone pine duff
release a quickening incense

A shy bird I've wanted to see for years
a wryneck, rare woodpecker
who plucks ants from the floor

and whose head swivels like an owl's
regards me sideways from a pine

then flies off a little way and looks back
over her shoulder like a Vermeer girl

Mountain rain

We thought the old cherry
dead when they pollard cut it
then last year's growth tendrilled
and the serins hot on nesting
swirled around its blossoms

The density of the rain's music
as it holds a shifting curtain
showmanlike before the mountain
varies in rhyme with the images
its drops inscribe on the eye

Torn by the drops
like flags by artillery
petals fall

Green luminosity

Green luminosity—why is
sunlight through foliage
so moving?

It has been all my life

Perhaps
the way it renders clear
for a moment

the pulse
of life to these mortal
eyes giving them the view
the gods have always

The stone and the lichen

The stone whispers
low, soft, and slow
to the lichen

that spreads over
it like a skin
conjuring of light and water
threads that dissolve it
for ten thousand years

and the stone says
to the lichen:
ravish me

Turtle

Reliably each spring
out of the mud

crawls the turtle
onto his rock

in the river's crook
below our house

The rock is far enough
and sunsoaked

to make it the right place
for warming the blood

away from dog barks
and boys' easy reach

The turtle's main antagonist
a boy with a brain tumour

was helicoptered out for surgery
then gone

The turtle wasn't there this year
no one knows why

A reed

When you next watch a reed in the river
its reflection poised, angled
across the water's slipping face

let there be no room
between you two
for beauty to enter into

After a long illness

after a long illness
and its unwanted exploration
of being decades older

senses returning mind returning
humour comes out from hiding
body demands love again

seeing wildflowers
thronging the Pyrenees
surrounded by butterflies

able to fill your lungs
and remember their names

Eyne Valley

Is it neurotransmitters fill the body
with benevolence after two days
of Pyrenean mountain walks?

Do the long muscles' movements
ease away the daily stress?

Or is it the more direct magic
that enters through the eyes?

Blue silhouette of deadly
           monkshood against a silver stream
Goshawks chanting at treeline
            apart from the kettling raptors
A marsh frog offering the sun
           his permeable skin
And the ghostly bee magnet
              the best named on the mountain
            the wolfsbane
              poisonous too

Broomrape

Broomrape's pushing up
like stalks of leafless orchids

reddish yellow, many bloomed
hard to focus at one glance

and a parasite on vetch
A measure of the pulse

in these hills that there's
a lot of it around: only in

a rich and fecund place do
so many parasites thrive

Unbuckling

In a nearby field
two hundred orchids
unbuckle their seductive
blooms

For the bees
and hoverflies it's
like getting shore
leave after six
months at sea

One day a great squealing

Jennifer, she was to us, big and smart
Our village dog friend Bernie

didn't mind when we stopped to feed her
windfall fruit, carrying it up

to her pen in the valley cleft
where ducks are farmed

away from eyes and regulations
and a there's a decomposing caravan

for youthful trysting. Jennifer was grateful
for pears, apples and dinner ends

Then one day a great squealing
Her cries filled the hills as she ran

already far from her familiar pen
paysans in loud pursuit

We cheered her on hoping escape
would open onto freedom

But there are traditions here
and so the narrative

was set and then
the local tables

Heat

Drowned red petals of poppy
and carmine of rose

green of lost leaves
cerise of dropped cherries

more gorgeous all than tapestry
and under them

with lancelike precision
the snake, washed down

with the rest, to the end
of the canal

its surface organic and silky
as the petals ripple in

the air infrayellow with the
untraviolet pouring down

Entering

their edges   move sinuous
the curtains   overlapping up
two arms of an   octopus
entering   the room

upstairs   early evening
the warmth   left over
as you enter   its embrace
as in a patch   of lake
you swim into   from chill

Call

the liquid call
from the trees—
a golden oriole

the river below
carries me
away

A single walk

A single walk
where things live wild
and I'm subtly improved

A thousand walks
through this same place
and it's teaching still

Fête

At the village fête
the rock band
plays a quiet concert
for the elders at 7 pm

By 11 the mountain rock and disco
start to throb and the kids of summer
manoeuvre on the local square
with plastic cups of wine

By 3:30 am the church bell is
sounding with hammers
and in our close couples
snog and pee

Somewhere along the way
the kids visit compounds
where hunting dogs stay
and set them free

This morning two boys and a girl
giggle up from the mill pond
and a muscled hunting dog
trots over to visit

Help with plot

It's a hot August and we're both writing books
I'm downstairs at the table

Every day a little English girl whose family
has a place in the village

comes by, looks in the screen door
and asks if she can come in

to hear what I'm writing that day
She listens then tells me it's not very good

and suggests her edits
Although her plot lines don't work for me

I always look forward to next day's visit

From the desk looking out at the valley

What blots this whiteness
is not words
but renewal
the stem cells of meaning
beyond knowing's edge
multiplying unaided
tended

Drop of sweat

I've found a fine meadow far up
looking out on six ranges of mountains

It had been a vineyard, thousands
of hand laid stones holding terraces

beyond the village, each stone's
placement the living record

of a human drop of sweat
The meadow was made by pulling

up the vines, as I watched happening
in a field by the river

There's been an EU subsidy
to uproot them. We've had

says Guide Michelin, an embarrassing
overproduction in the region

The floods

The spring floods were great
this year, washing out
the road to the swimming hole

In the hills old drystone
walls holding empty
terraces gave way

They've scraped off the tumbled
remains. There's no one
left to mend them

At the top of the valley
on a cedar sits a short-toed
eagle, the feathers of its head

plumped to fullness. It flies
toward us and circles three
times then catches thermals

and shows the right wing
missing a secondary feather
as it crests the ridge

The cherry orchard

Our nearest neighbour, called
'your crazy neighbour' by our
other neighbours, has died
while we were away
She'd lived in care some years

We'd thought of buying a small
terrace from her, below our house
We'd grown a cherry orchard
down there by tossing over
pits from the sweetest trees

Her children have returned
to the house and celebrated her
memory by chopping down the
cherry orchard. In its corner

grew calla lilies which she'd
climb down to reach each spring
while she could and we'd do it
for her later. She'd lay them on

her husband's grave in the
village graveyard. Looking down
just now I saw a calla blooming

Encarmined

Hugo our companion
whom we call Bernie
has been taking us on hill walks
fourteen years

It wasn't just the lamb fat
pâté or occasional foie gras
we slipped him

This week we noticed he was left behind
when the men took the younger dogs
off to hunt

He was too old, said the villagers
so we took him on a walk
Bernie disappeared down a gorge
into the garrigue and after a sound of thrashing
a wild boar screamed long and hard

When all was quiet
Bernie came back encarmined
bathed in contentment
boar's blood dripping from his muzzle

We told the village and next
morning the lead jeep heading
out to hunt had Bernie

riding shot gun. He looked
at us with pride and we both
believe we saw him wink

Anniversary

Outside our window this hot August
the golden oriole is practising
liquescent scales

The swallowtail caterpillar, golden
washed fritillaries, crimson and
black true bugs and mating beetles
the asp viper pushing up
from the canal and absorbing
itself into the rock

the intense small ants
pulling peanut fragments
into their nest

during our apero
on the terrace while house martins
roost on the wire

five years
                our life
                        today

in the life of all life

Cave coopérative

We've been communards here a long time
When we came the cépage, the time
they pick the grapes, seemed
something to join in, and the wine
from the cave coopérative
would wash dinner down

Then we learned our communal wine
went into industrial alcohol
and just a few old men
still drank their own

One brought us into his garage
He crushed grapes in an ancient
wooden tub, working with pride
surrounded by a thick fug
of solvent and petrol fumes

Now the local vines produce
for a young neighbour, son of the old mayor
He makes wine the latest biodynamic way
It's wine you'd have luck to drink every day
wine that makes you proud
to be a communard

Sugar cubes

Middle of August and thirty-eight
centigrade, the wind blowing
hot perfume, atomized oil
from thyme, lavender and obscurer
favourites, into my face
as I wash the dishes of midday
hake with three kinds of wine
and remember ants

Though colonies live only a few years
a convoy has ceaselessly worked
along our terrace fence these
eighteen and when we didn't
bag the sugar cubes before leaving
returned in spring to a hundred
perfectly wrapped cubes
with nothing inside

Living with Don Quixote

The Don lives close enough to La Mancha
on the shelf in our village house

He's been meeting me here more than ten years
every visit I make and I'm less than halfway

Whatever Harold Bloom and the other critics say
it's glacial for me

And when I'm done and the confused knight retires
for good to the shelf

many years from now then perhaps like Pierre Menard
in Borges, I'll write his story

from scratch and it will come out
word for word the original

Scarab: *Hoplia coerulea*

Cross river and climb rocks to find it
painted with the sky this beetle

More vivid than anything by Fabergé
and you cannot own it as it crawls away

Imagine holding a live cerulean scarab
let its sorcery in

> If you have a vision as you lay dying
> your strivings recessed to mind's perimeter
>
> will you see nature spinning its unneeded
> beauty of form and movement of song and taste
>
> > If so and had you the luck to meet it
> > such a beetle might guide you
> >
> > to the value of your leaving life
> > and to the next

These wrinkles

These wrinkles are a gift
these aches a joyous sign

that I am here now
that life lives me now

This is the now shape
this is the way

While on holiday

While on holiday in our cave
I overheard us talking
about where we wanted
to live in twenty years

As I take the Eurostar back
to London I recall this twenty
years, a temporal lobe
of love's body, and the neutral

tone of our discussion as in
would you like more tea
and know that we'll always
be together somewhere

Niaux

Our guide was a tough young
Gitane smoking anthropologist

A kilometre into the cave
We followed her torch

to a round space like a chapel
She played the light

on bison and horses
running across the living rock

for the past four hundred
generations

We stood long and softly walked
a kilometre back

emerged as from a birth canal
with tears

Feast of amphibians

Fourteen months away
autumn pours down as we drive in at night
car lips the crest into the valley
the point of threshold

hundreds of toads on the road
a wet world more welcoming
after a bone dry summer
and so a careful drive

Large and stately marching slow
fire salamanders yellow and indigo
nine this evening come and go
just three in the prior years of hoping so

Moving at mammal speed a genet
wild forbears brought by Saracens
a thousand years ago
ocelot to a quick view
but their own genus and wild still
out for a feast of amphibians

In the morning's heavy rain a heron
river running full throated
wings over its waters
a sharp eye for toads still roaming
disappears in mist

Fourteen months away
and coming back is
being back

Endurance

It's New Year's Day in the village
and an old lady friend
wearing a new sweater
lets me buzz her on the cheeks

I tell her she looks good
and she says, "yes, we must
make the most of life
for it is so very short"

Winter reveals
the endurance of things

our vivid brevity

Also from Barbican Press
James Thornton's *The Feynman Challenge*

'In this unusual and exceptionally interesting work, James Thornton speaks as both a poet who has colonized science and a scientist who speaks a poetic tongue.' – *Edward O. Wilson, University Professor Emeritus, Harvard University, double Pulitzer Prize winner*

'A brilliant introduction to the endless wonders of our universe, from quantum levels to the cosmos. It opened my eyes to many marvels and oddities.' – *Eberhard Fetz, Professor of Physiology & Biophysics, University of Washington*

'Poets sometimes flinch at the idea of footnotes. Poems, they think, should be perfect small worlds of their own. The Feynman Challenge upends this aesthetic. Like the Pompidou Centre, it wears all its workings on the outside. Plunging into the sea of scientific knowledge, it comes up grinning and glittering with droplets of lovely information. It is a generous book, happy to serve the curiosity, the wonder and humility of science, happening here and there in words that simply send a shudder – *Two black holes are about / to marry, a billion years ago* – through our sense of time and space.' – *Philip Gross, winner of the T.S.Eliot Prize*